PROGRESSIVE ROCK GUITAR LICKS

Full Length Video, Plus Book, Includes More Than 60 Adventurous Phrases!

by Chris Letchford

To access video and audio visit:
www.halleonard.com/mylibrary
Enter Code
4330-5708-5768-8984

ISBN 978-1-4950-1157-3

HAL•LEONARD®
CORPORATION
7777 W. BLUEMOUND RD. P.O. BOX 13819 MILWAUKEE, WI 53213

In Australia Contact:
Hal Leonard Australia Pty. Ltd.
4 Lentara Court
Cheltenham, Victoria, 3192 Australia
Email: ausadmin@halleonard.com.au

Copyright © 2015 by HAL LEONARD CORPORATION
International Copyright Secured   All Rights Reserved

No part of this publication may be reproduced in any form or by
any means without the prior written permission of the Publisher.

Visit Hal Leonard Online at
www.halleonard.com

TABLE OF CONTENTS

INTRODUCTION 4

HOW TO USE
THIS BOOK 4

ABOUT THE AUTHOR . 4

A MAJOR 5
   LICK #1 5
   LICK #2 5

A MINOR 6
   LICK #3 6
   LICK #4 6
   LICK #5 7

A♭ MAJOR 7
   LICK #6 7
   LICK #7 8
   LICK #8 8

B♭ MINOR 9
   LICK #9 9
   LICK #10 9
   LICK #11 10

B♭ MIXOLYDIAN 10
   LICK #12 10
   LICK #13 11
   LICK #14 11

C MAJOR 12
   LICK #15 12
   LICK #16 12
   LICK #17 13

C MINOR 13
   LICK #18 13
   LICK #19 14
   LICK #20 14
   LICK #21 15

D HARMONIC
MINOR 15
   LICK #22 15
   LICK #23 16

D MAJOR 16
   LICK #24 16
   LICK #25 17
   LICK #26 17

C♯ MINOR 18
   LICK #27 18
   LICK #28 18
   LICK #29 19
   LICK #30 19
   LICK #31 20
   LICK #32 20

E LYDIAN 21
   LICK #33 21
   LICK #34 21
   LICK #35 22

E PHRYGIAN 22
   LICK #36 22
   LICK #37 23
   LICK #38 23

F MAJOR 24
   LICK #39 24
   LICK #40 24

F MINOR 25
   LICK #41 25
   LICK #42 25
   LICK #43 26

B LYDIAN 26
   LICK #44 26
   LICK #45 27
   LICK #46 27

G DORIAN 28
   LICK #47 28
   LICK #48 29
   LICK #49 30

G MAJOR 30
   LICK #50 30
   LICK #51 31
   LICK #52 31

G♭ LYDIAN 32
   LICK #53 32
   LICK #54 32
   LICK #55 33

BONUS SECTION:
SEVEN-STRING
GUITAR 34

A MINOR 34
   LICK #56 34

B♭ MIXOLYDIAN 35
   LICK #57 35

C MAJOR 35
   LICK #58 35

C MINOR 36
   LICK #59 36

B LYDIAN 36
   LICK #60 36

D HARMONIC
MINOR 37
   LICK #61 37

D MAJOR 37
   LICK #62 37

E LYDIAN 38
   LICK #63 38

G♭ LYDIAN 39
   LICK #64 39

G MAJOR 40
   LICK #65 40

INTRODUCTION

Welcome to Chris Letchford's *Progressive Rock Guitar Licks*. This book is aimed at intermediate to advanced guitar players looking to learn and add some unique and modern guitar licks to strengthen their soloing vocabulary.

Throughout the book you'll learn licks that feature one of the many guitar techniques needed to be a well rounded guitar player, including: tapping, string skipping, arpeggios, vibrato, string bending, hammer-ons/pull-offs, slides, grace notes, legato, speed bursts, staccato, palm muting, and sweep picking.

HOW TO USE THIS BOOK

Each lick is played on the video two times. The first time is at regular speed; listen and follow along in the book. The second time is slow so you can play along with it. The slow version is preceded by count-off clicks, indicated in the book, so you know when to come in. Once you've mastered the lick, play along with the backing tracks using the licks provided, or play your own and improvise.

These modern backing tracks feature a great mix of keys, rhythms, and tempos to play the licks and melodies over, and also to further practice your improvising. All tracks were written, recorded, mixed, and mastered by John Browne of the band Monuments.

ABOUT THE AUTHOR

Chris Letchford has been playing music for twenty-two years and guitar for the last seventeen years. He has released four instructional books, teaches clinics, and tours full time with his band Scale the Summit. Chris is also a solo artist and session player, having won multiple awards for his guitar playing and has been featured in many of the top guitar magazines. He currently resides in Pagosa Springs, CO living on his mountain property with his wife and two Great Danes.

A MAJOR 🔊 1

▶ LICK #1

This first lick explores the entire fingerboard while applying a mixture of 16th-note phrasing, slides, and arpeggios within the key.

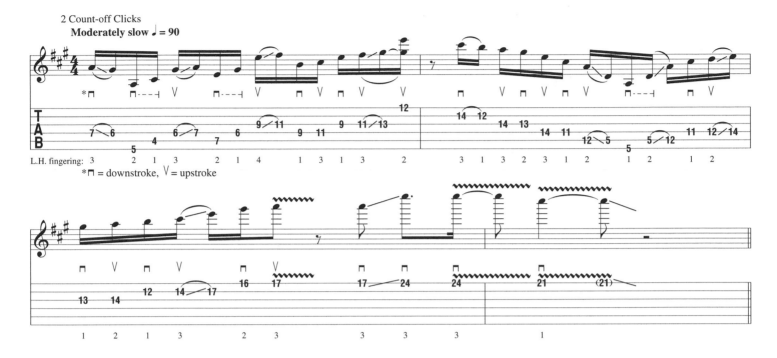

▶ LICK #2

This next lick uses a mixture of string skipping, hammer-ons/pull-offs, bends, and grace notes. That's the key to writing really dynamic licks and leads—having a good mix of techniques.

A MINOR 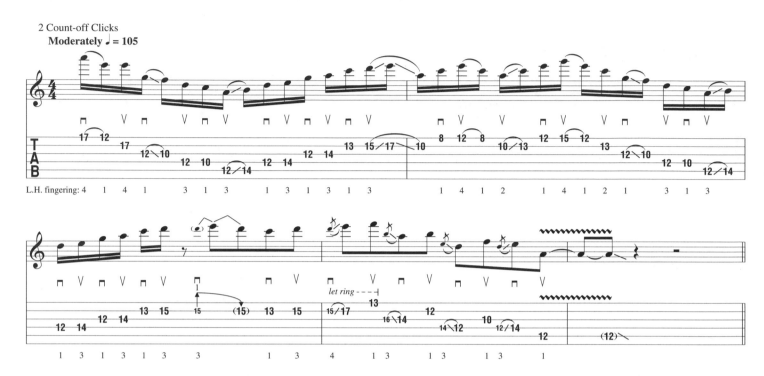 2

▶ LICK #3
This lick uses unique arpeggio shapes from the key.

▶ LICK #4
This lick uses legato technique and slides to create a melodic phrase.

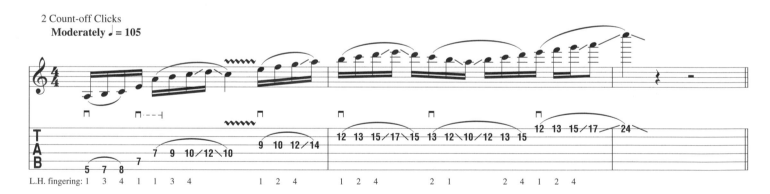

LICK #5

The approach of this lick is "less is more." Sometimes the most vocal guitar leads are the simplest ones. This lick uses a mixture of hammer-ons, grace notes, and vibrato.

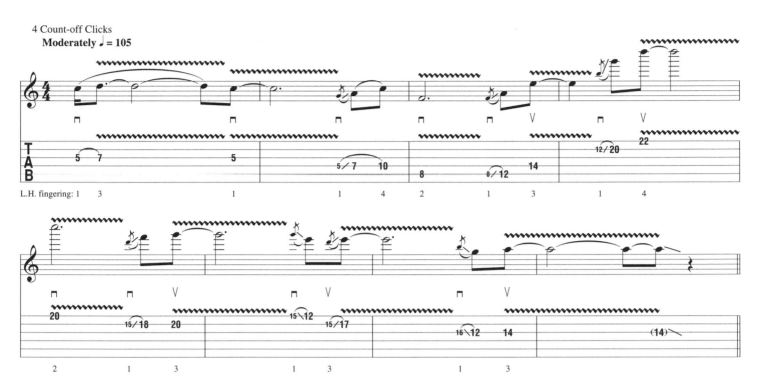

A♭ MAJOR 3

 ## LICK #6

Using a wide range of sounds, this lick explores the use of grace notes, slides, arpeggios, speed bursts, and hammer-ons.

LICK #7

This lick was written with tapping technique as the key focus while still maintaining a very melodic sound.

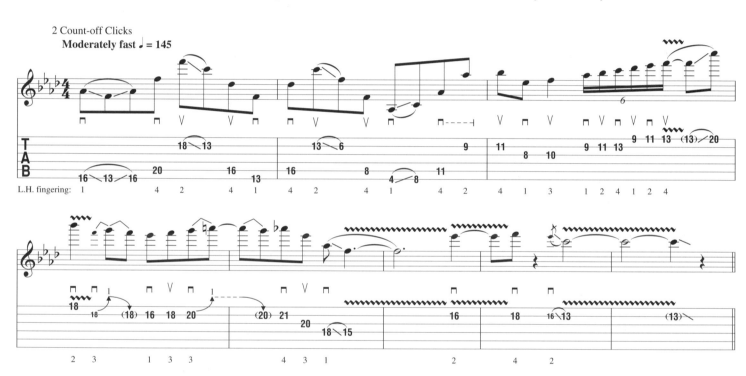

LICK #8

This next lick uses string skipping, shred runs, and bends to create a very melodic phrase.

B♭ MINOR 4

 LICK #9

This lick is written with a traditional string-skipping approach. The bulk of the movement is in the higher register but it still creates a unique melody by placing the movements in an out-of-the-ordinary spot within each bar.

 LICK #10

This next lick uses the hammer-on technique of the fretting hand while tapping with the picking hand.

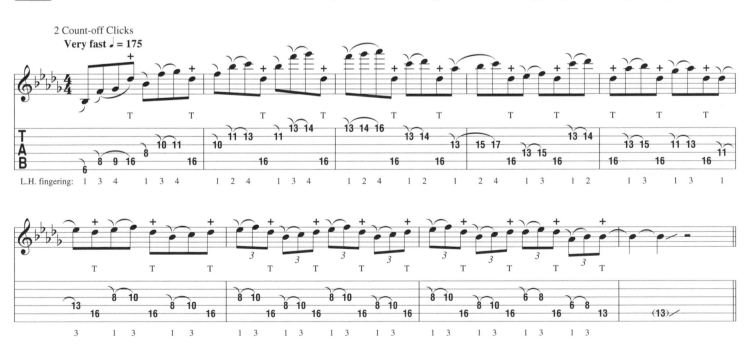

LICK #11

While using the notes of the Bb minor scale, this lick steps "outside" in measure 2 via the raised (major) 7th, briefly implying the Bb harmonic minor scale.

Bb MIXOLYDIAN 5

LICK #12

This lick mainly focuses on staccato but also includes a few bends, pull-offs, and slides.

LICK #13

This next lick is played with tapping technique while also combining string skipping and legato technique from the fret hand.

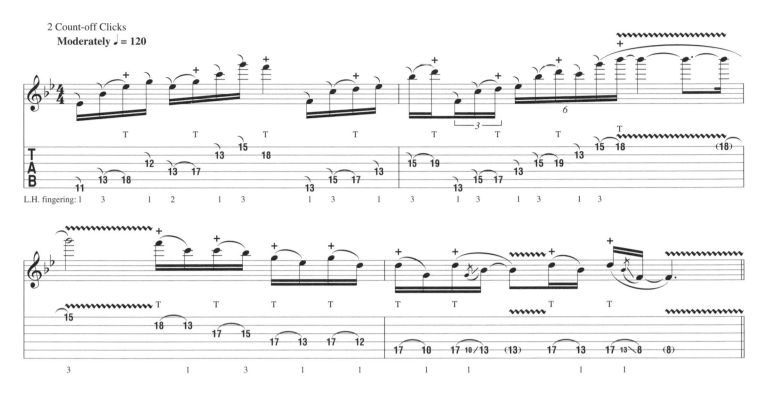

LICK #14

This is the most melodic phrasing of the B♭ Mixolydian licks, using a combination of arpeggios, slides, pull-offs, bends, and palm muting. Pay close attention to the notes that need to be held towards the end of the first measure (see "let ring").

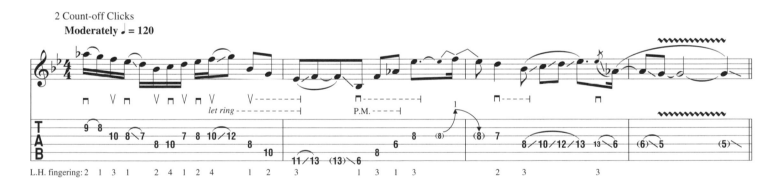

C MAJOR 6

 LICK #15

Tapping is the goal of this lick, which explores the use of descending arpeggios inside of the key while tapping the higher pitches.

 LICK #16

This next lick is built upon one continuous, unique arpeggio inside of the key.

LICK #17

This lick focuses on slide technique. In measures 4–7, an off-beat feel is created by the odd grouping of notes inside of the arpeggios.

C MINOR 🔊 7

 ## LICK #18

This next lick combines multiple techniques (pull-offs, slides, arpeggios, grace notes, bends, and vibrato) to form a very melodic and dark phrase inside of the key.

LICK #19

This is another "less is more"-style lick that really sings along with the backing riff. Pay close attention to the longer vibrato, making sure that it's in time with the song, as well as to the fast bends near the end, making sure to reach the pitch of each.

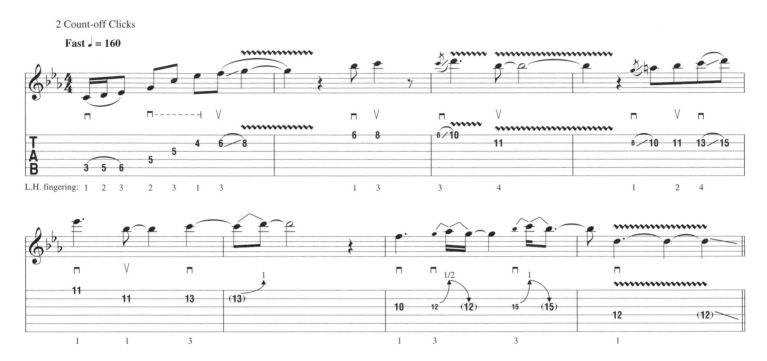

 8

 LICK #20

This next lick uses a multitude of techniques to form a melodic phrase, and introduces some syncopated five-note runs in measure 3.

14

LICK #21

Tapping technique is used once again, but this lick really varies how the tapping note is used to connect with the fretted note (i.e., with pull-offs, hammer-ons, and/or string skipping).

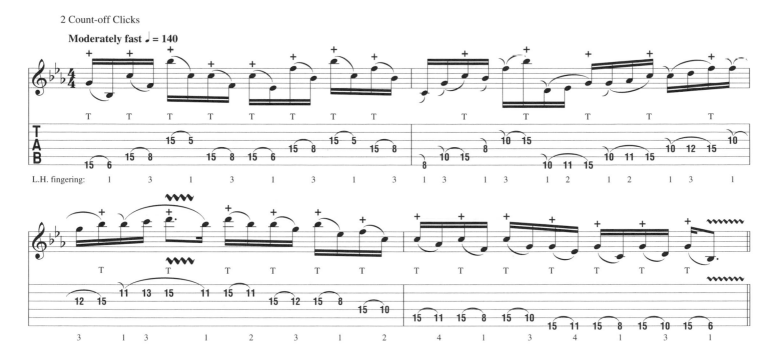

D HARMONIC MINOR 9

LICK #22

This lick uses speed bursts in combination with sweep picking. Pay close attention to the number of notes in each pattern since it rotates between five and four.

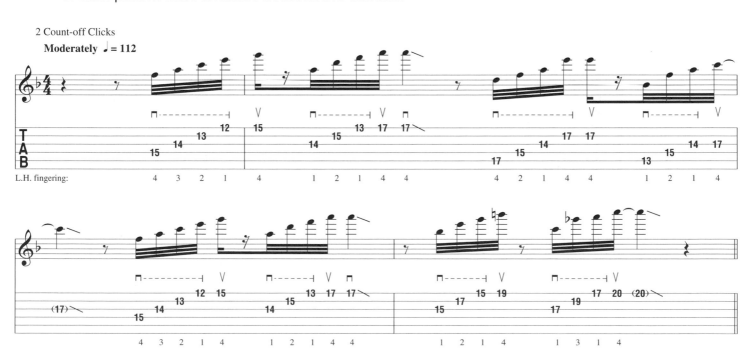

LICK #23

This next lick explores the more traditional scale runs found in the metal genre while still having a unique sound and fitting very well with the backing track.

D MAJOR 10

LICK #24

This lick should be approached as a melodic complement to the overall song, rather than as an upfront lead or lick. This D major phrase uses the common tapping/pull-off technique to create that interesting, fast high- to low-register melody.

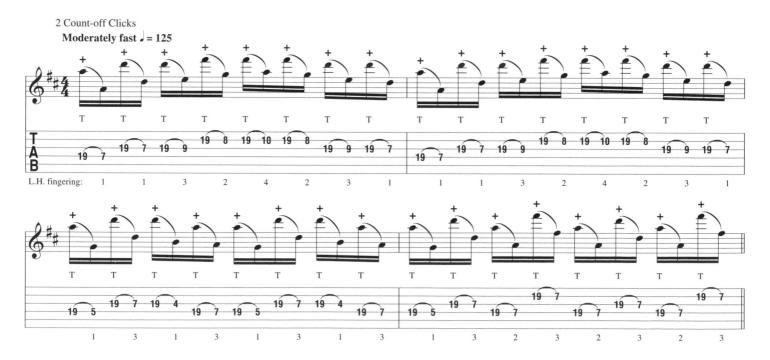

▶ LICK #25

This next lick uses arpeggios, speed bursts, and long vibrato to create an interesting phrase.

▶ LICK #26

This is the last of the D major licks. It really focuses heavily on bending technique, combined with tapping.

Pro tip: There are multiple options for switching from picking to tapping in quick runs like this. If you watch in the video, I prefer to switch my pick to my middle finger, as it makes it easier to mute the unused open strings by keeping the palm flat. Using the middle finger to tap also works, if that's what you are used to, but with respect to long-term technical benefits, I recommend the "swap technique" that I used in this lick/video.

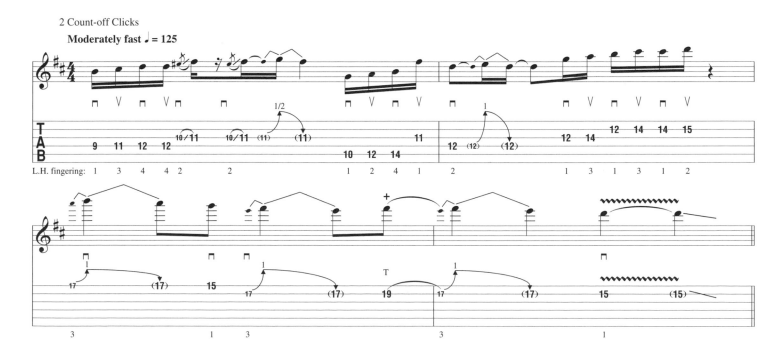

C# MINOR 11

LICK #27

This first C# minor lick uses bends, slides, grace notes, pull-offs, and the always-interesting dotted notes (quarter and eighth) to create a unique and dark phrase. Pay close attention to the sweep-picking run in the second measure.

LICK #28

This lick focuses on the use of space between runs, which really helps to create an interesting phrasing dynamic for lead guitar. Although in the key of C# minor, the lick still has a very melodic and happy sound to it.

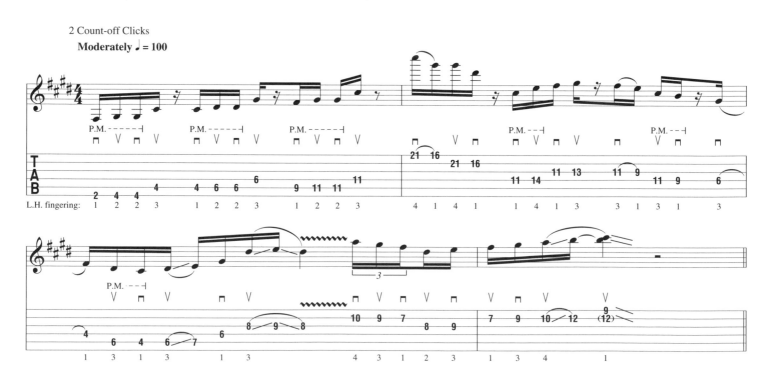

18

LICK #29

This melodic lick combines string skipping, slides, bends, palm muting, grace notes, and vibrato—the key to creating great melodic phrases.

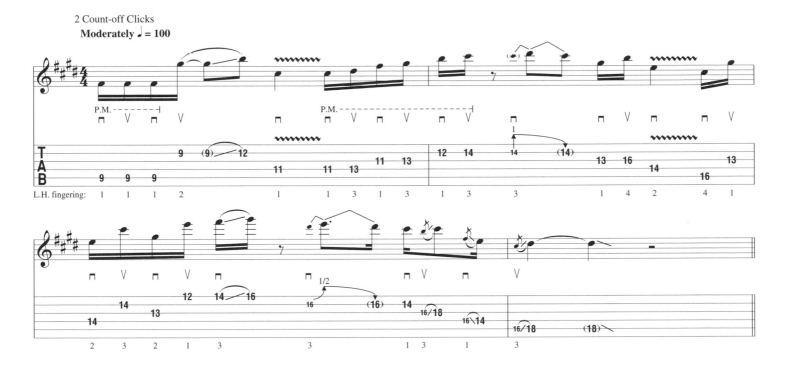

LICK #30

This lick uses a common technique found in a lot of Scale the Summit songs: double picking. This phrase would classify more as a riff than a lick, but it still has that upfront, lead sound to it.

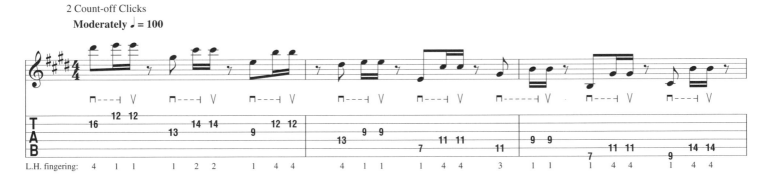

LICK #31

This lick uses tapping technique and triplets. Some of the phrasing involves triplets grouped in sets of four notes, resulting in a unique, outside-of-the-box approach.

LICK #32

This last C♯ minor lick uses a "continuous run" approach that makes for a very climactic theme while also challenging the player since there is little room for second guessing what is being played.

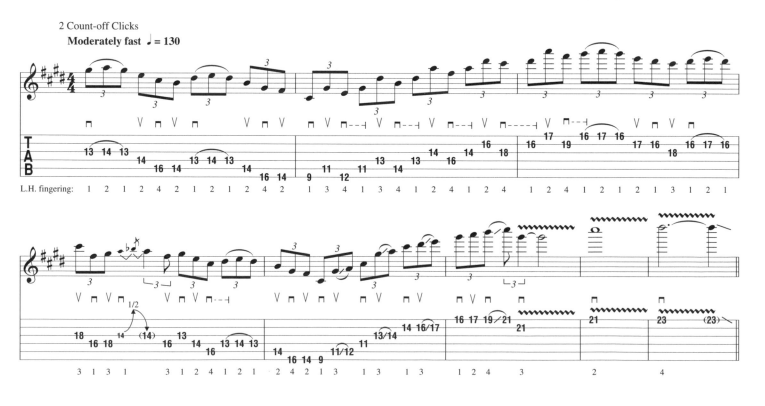

E LYDIAN 🔊 13

LICK #33

This first E Lydian lick focuses on a wide variety of techniques, including pull-offs, vibrato, string skipping, staccato, grace notes, and slides.

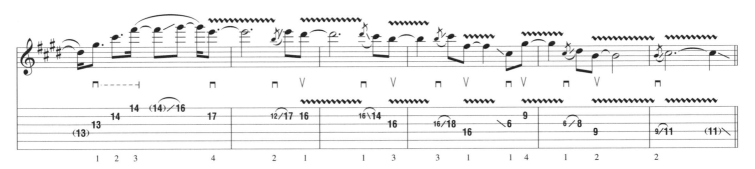

LICK #34

This lick uses what many tend to leave out of their solos: chords. Make sure to play close attention to the held notes in measures 5–7. Chords can make for an interesting harmonic layer over the existing backing-track chords.

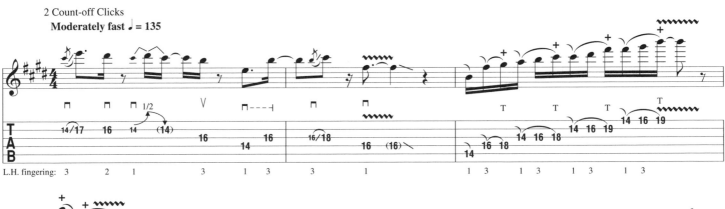

LICK #35

This last E Lydian lick focuses on open strings. Be sure to keep the open string from ringing out when moving to the next string.

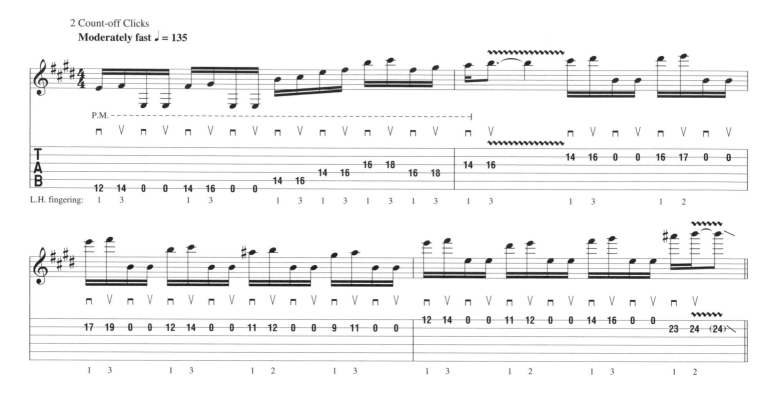

E PHRYGIAN 14

LICK #36

This lick uses some original E Phrygian arpeggio shapes across the fingerboard to form a very dark yet melodic phrase.

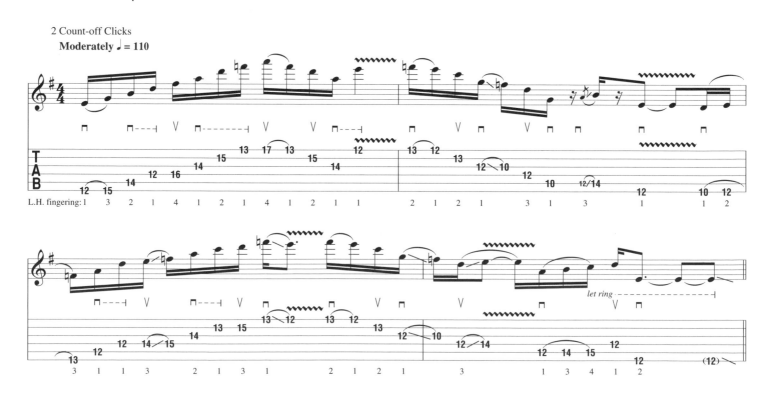

LICK #37

This next lick combines diatonic (inside of the key) arpeggios and tapping.

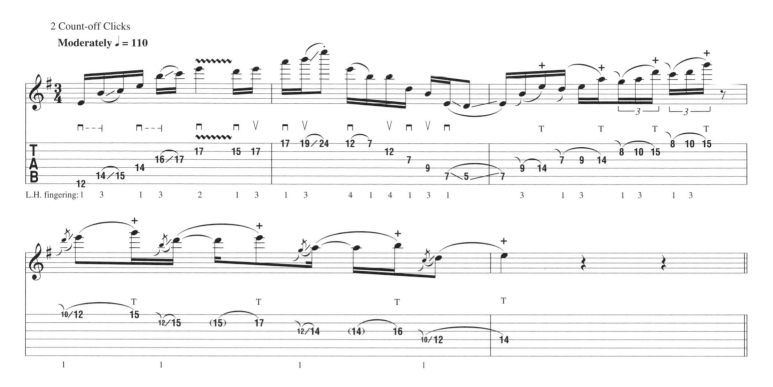

LICK #38

This last E Phrygian lick uses ascending runs found in a lot of metal solos—very fitting for the overall Phrygian vibe.

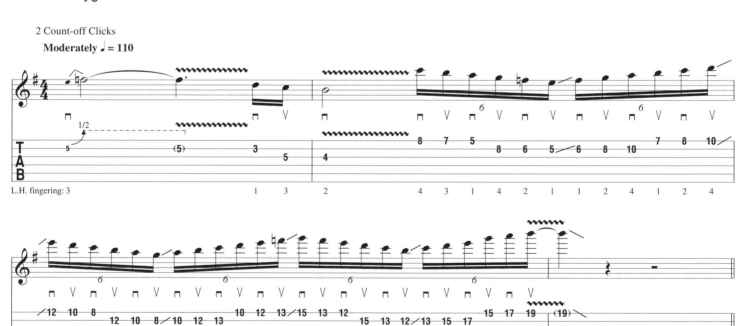

F MAJOR 15

▶ LICK #39

This first F major lick uses (long) slide technique. Make sure to fully mute (rest) in-between each two-note slide; it helps with the overall dynamics of the lick.

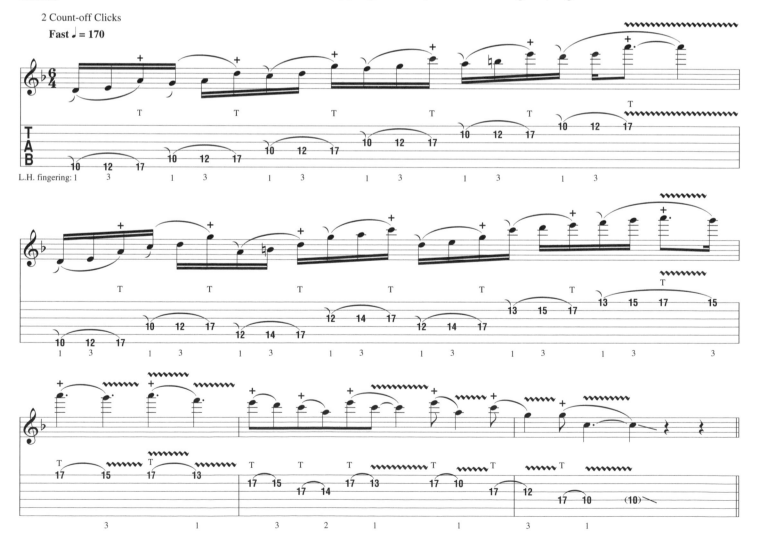

▶ LICK #40

This next lick uses a mixture of different tapping techniques and note groupings.

F MINOR 🔊 16

▶ LICK #41

This lick uses chord-soloing technique in combination with sweep picking and descending scale runs. Pay close attention to the proper picking technique for this lick.

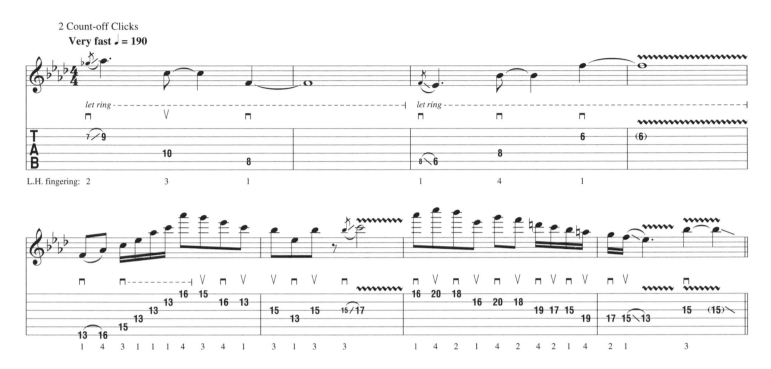

▶ LICK #42

This next lick focuses on mixing many techniques to form one dynamic phrase. Make sure the quick bends in measures 5–6 are bent to pitch (these are easy to under-bend since they move so fast).

LICK #43

This last F minor lick combines diatonic arpeggios, hammer-ons, legato, slides, rests, and speed bursts.

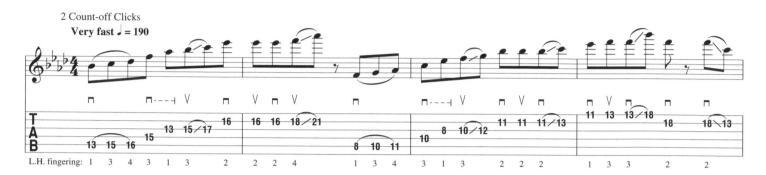

B LYDIAN 17

 LICK #44

This first B Lydian lick uses a wide range of sliding techniques. The focus here is using lots of dynamics to create a very melodic run.

LICK #45

This is another lick that could be easily classified as a riff, but chords can be used as a lead guitar technique, as well, which you'll see with this one.

LICK #46

This last B Lydian lick puts to work fast alternate picking for some speed-burst runs. This approach is a great technique for the final moments of a solo, when you're looking for that very climactic ending.

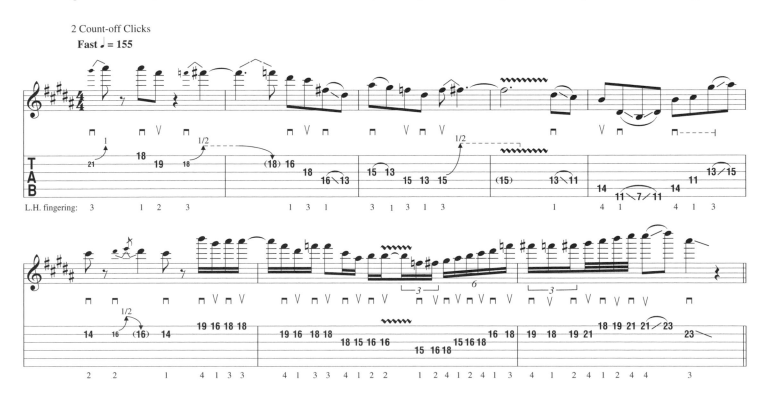

G DORIAN 18

LICK #47

This G Dorian lick showcases the use of five-note groupings within the sweep shapes while also incorporating speed bursts, bends, and vibrato.

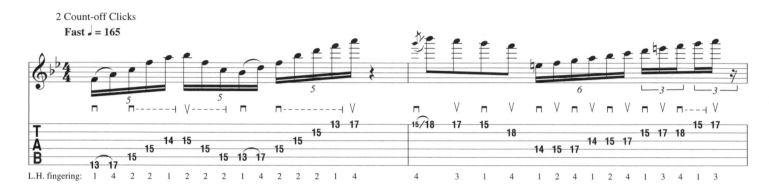

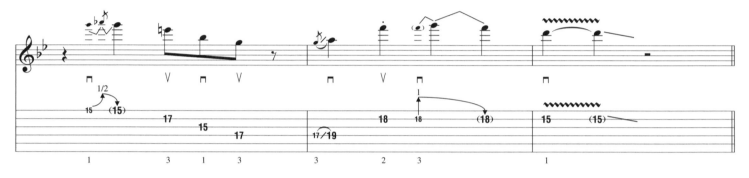

LICK #48

This lick showcases phrasing and how it works over multiple changes using slides, grace notes, string skipping, bends, and rakes.

LICK #49

This last G Dorian lick uses shifting slides, bends, vibrato, and grace notes.

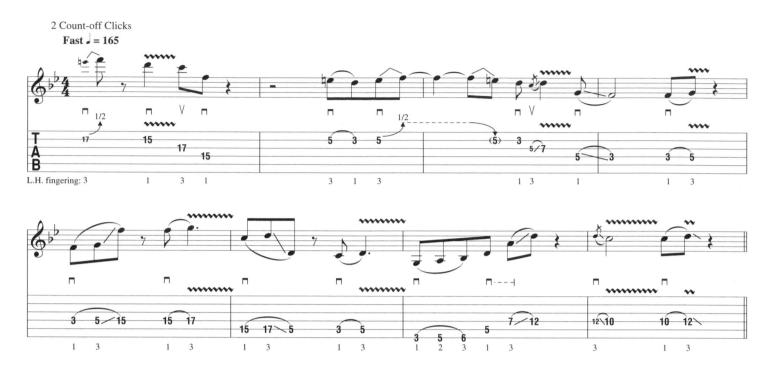

G MAJOR 19

LICK #50

This first G major lick incorporates string skipping, slides, bends, hammer-ons, and some beat displacement.

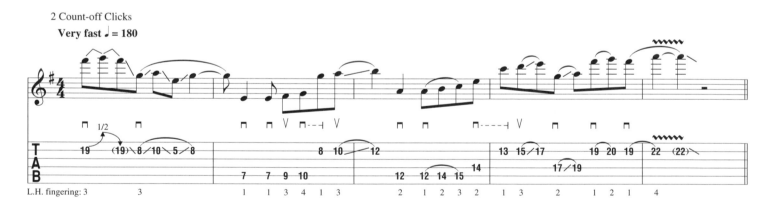

LICK #51

This next lick showcases the use of chords for lead guitar. Pay close attention to the notes that need to be held, which are indicated by the "let ring" instruction between the tab and notation staves.

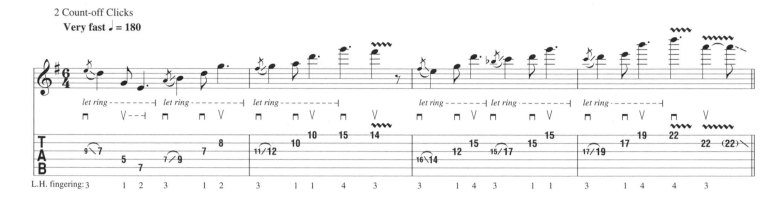

LICK #52

This last G Major lick focuses on different types of speed bursts while still maintaining the melodic lead structure.

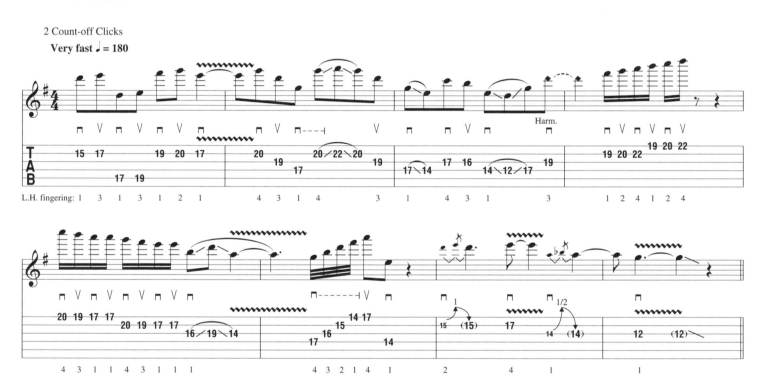

G♭ LYDIAN 20

LICK #53
This first G♭ Lydian lick uses a "continuous run" approach while incorporating really fast position shifts via slides.

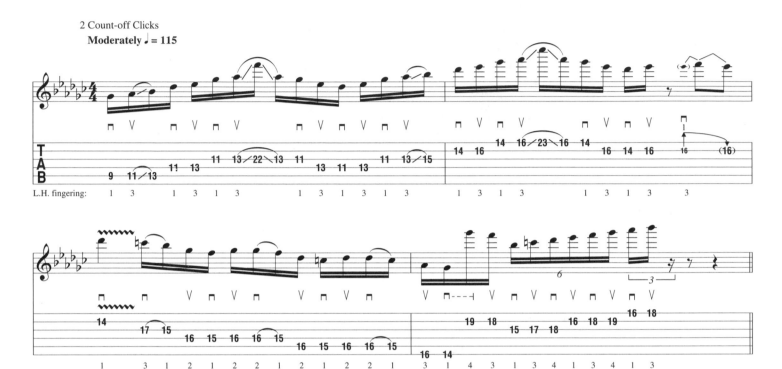

LICK #54
This lick uses some original G♭ Lydian arpeggio shapes across the fingerboard to form the very distinctive sound of the Lydian mode.

LICK #55

This last G♭ Lydian lick combines traditional metal guitar with sliding double stops, which are commonly found in the blues genre.

2 Count-off Clicks

Moderately ♩ = 115

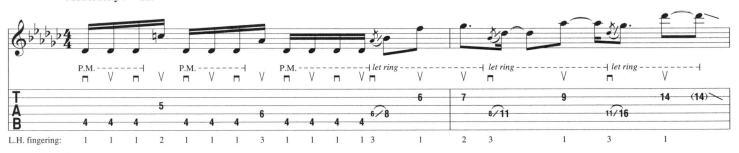

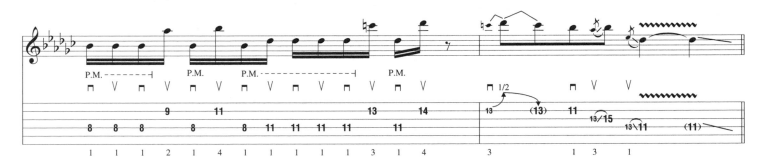

BONUS SECTION: SEVEN-STRING GUITAR

All licks incorporate all seven strings of a standard-tuned seven-string guitar.

A MINOR 2

LICK #56

This A minor lick incorporates seven-string arpeggios, slides, grace notes, string skipping, and legato.

Bb MIXOLYDIAN 5

▶ LICK #57
This next lick focuses on arpeggios, palm muting, string skipping, scale runs, and vibrato.

C MAJOR 6

▶ LICK #58
This next lick uses bends, open strings, pull-offs, slides, and the full range of the fingerboard.

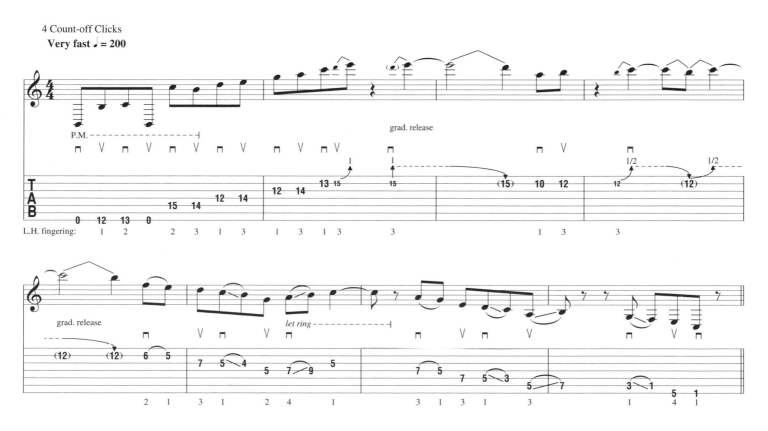

C MINOR 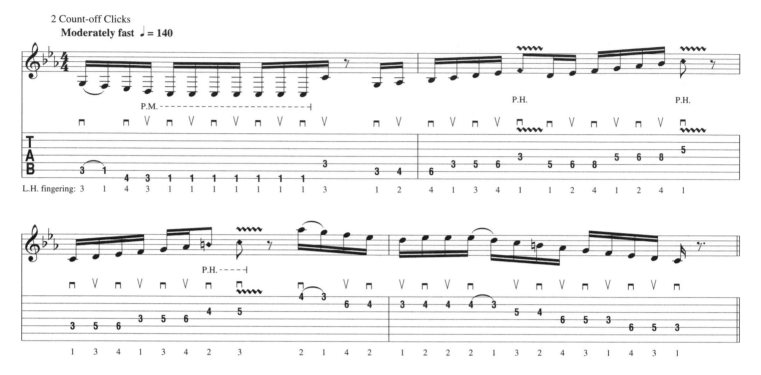 8

▶ LICK #59

This next lick uses a more traditional metal approach, incorporating palm muting, scale runs, and pinch harmonics.

B LYDIAN ◀ 17

▶ LICK #60

This lick uses ascending fifths predominantly, along with bends, slides, and vibrato.

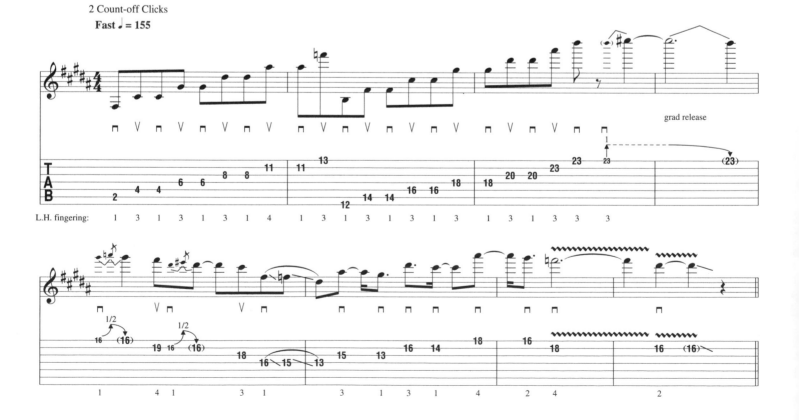

D HARMONIC MINOR 9

LICK #61

This lick also uses a traditional metal approach, incorporating scale runs, slides, and speed bursts.

4 Count-off Clicks
Very fast ♩ = 225

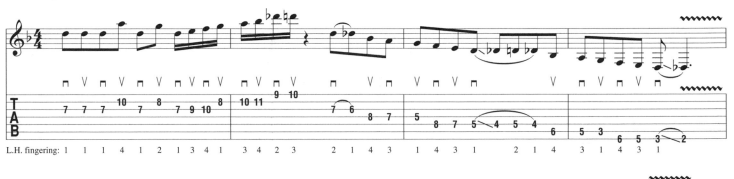

D MAJOR 🔊 10

LICK #62

This next lick uses double picking as its main theme, along with string skipping and vibrato.

2 Count-off Clicks
Moderately fast ♩ = 125

E LYDIAN 🔊 13

▶ LICK #63
This lick utilizes open strings, grace notes, beat displacement, speed bursts, and vibrato to create a very unique and melodic phrase.

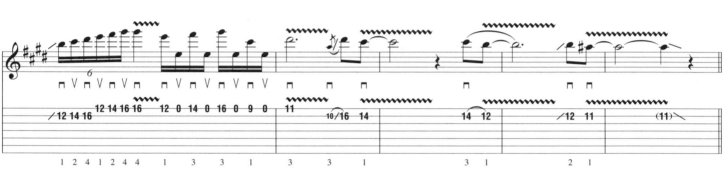

G♭ LYDIAN 20

LICK #64
This next lick uses what I like to call the "tongue twister" of guitar: mixing up the organization of descending scale shapes inside of the key.

G MAJOR  19

▶ LICK #65

This last lick uses slides, string skipping, grace notes, legato, vibrato, bends, and chords.